The Royal Naval ⎯⎯

Hornsea Mere
and
Killingholme
1914-1919

Photographs, documents, notes
and reminiscences
of 28348 G. T. W. Gelsthorpe
Air Mechanic First Class, R.N.A.S.

By Joe Gelsthorpe

© 2014

The Royal Naval Air Service at Hornsea and Killingholme 1914-1919
© Joe Gelsthorpe 2014
Compiled by Linda Ellis
Typeset by Mike Wilson

ISBN: 978-1-291-98513-9

First published in Great Britain by
Lodge Books 2014

25 South Back Lane
Bridlington
www.lodgebooks.co.uk

Heading 1917

Dedicated to my Father, Air Mechanic First Class 28348 Gladwin Thomas
Webster Gelsthorpe, of 248 Squadron R.N.A.S.

3

Preface

The Royal Naval Air Service was formed in 1914 then amalgamated with the Royal Flying Corps in 1918 to form the Royal Air Force.

In Hornsea, the aircraft were single-seater Sopwith Baby seaplanes (also known as floatplanes) and two-seater Short 184 seaplanes, which flew coastal patrols off the Yorkshire coast until the end of the war.

Contents

1. Introduction to G.T.W. in Civilian Life

Gladwin Thomas Webster Gelsthorpe (1890-1968), aged 27.

G. T. W. Gelsthorpe was born in Hucknall, Nottinghamshire, on 27th April 1890, the son of Thomas Gelsthorpe, a Master Joiner, and Kate (nee Webster), his wife.

They ran a house-building firm, building houses in Harehills, Leeds, and Bentley, near Doncaster.

G.T.W. was a time-served joiner and carpenter.

When the First World War started, they had enough rental income from property to retire and moved to Rose Cottage, Healing, Lincolnshire, where they opened a market garden.

Gladwin had to be registered under the National Registration Act, and his certificate is shown on the next page.

This Certificate must be signed and carefully preserved by the person to whom it is issued.

If the place of residence of the holder of the Certificate is changed otherwise than temporarily, the Certificate must within 28 days be handed in at a Post Office or sent or delivered to the Clerk of the Council of the Borough, Urban or Rural District in which the new residence is situate or, in Scotland, the Town or County Clerk), with the new address written in the space below. A fresh Certificate will be supplied in due course.

Space for new address

NATIONAL REGISTRATION ACT, 1915.

This is to Certify that

(a) Gladwin Gelsthorpe

(b) Joiner (25)

(c) of Rose Villa, Healing

has been Registered under the NATIONAL REGISTRATION ACT, 1915.

Signature of Holder. G. Gelsthorpe

GOD SAVE THE KING.

(a) Name. (b) Occupation. (c) Postal Address.

8

2. Joining Up Process and Entering the R.N.A.S.

After the war started, G.T.W. applied to join the forces. After not being called up for some time, villagers at Healing asked why. Various letters passed between G. T. W. and the recruiting office.

PUBLIC   NOTICE.

MR. G. GELSTHORPE wishes to thank his kind friend

(or friends) for their interest as regards his continued

residence in this Village.

The copy of letter attached will no doubt provide for

him, or them, the necessary information.

Royal Naval Air Service
Recruiting Office,
Crystal Palace, LONDON S.E.
Feb. 22nd 1917.

Mr. G. Gelsthorpe,
Rose Villa,
HEALING, Lincs.

Sir,
In reply to your postcard dated the 18th instant, you are informed that your enrolment in the R.N.A.S. Reserve on the 27/7/16 as 1st Grade Air Mechanic-(C) has not been overlooked, and you will be called up at a fortnight's notice when your services are required. Nothing can be stated, however, as to when this will be as no date has yet been fixed by the Admiralty.

Yours faithfully,

Flt. Lieut. R.N.,
for Commander (B).,
R.N. Air Service.

Ref. D.7263/1-EWC.

9

3. Training

On 26th March 1917, he was told to attend training for the R.N.A.S. (Royal Naval Air Service) at Crystal Palace, Norwood, London, at a rate of pay of 4s (20 pence) per day and, before his toolkit was passed, he had to purchase a metric rule and round-nosed parallel-grip pliers, which were used for wire rigging. He received a further 3d (2.08 pence) per day tool money. He learned aircraft construction and repair.

Above: Trainees.

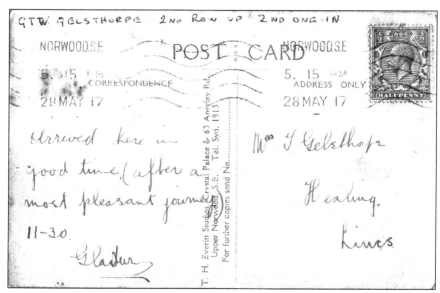

Above: He sent a card to his parents.

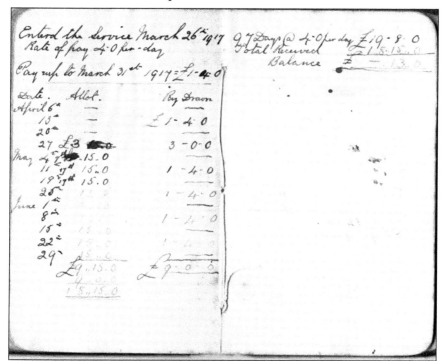

Above: An entry from his notebook on joining, showing his rate of pay.

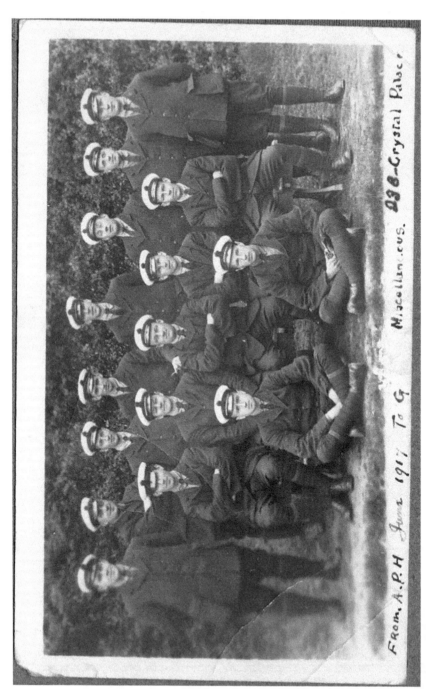

Above: Other trainees.

F. S. Form 19.

AIR FORCES.

RECORD OF CLOTHING ISSUED

TO

No. *227656*

Rank *1st Am.*

Name *Getchorn. G.*

Trade *Carpenter.*

Date of enlistment *26d March 1917*

GD833 200,000 1/18 HWV(P)

SCALE OF CLOTHING.

Ordinary Clothing			Working Clothing (a)		
Articles		No.	Articles		No.
Boots	.. prs.	2	Suits, combination	..	2
Caps	..	1			
Drawers	.. prs.	2	Motor Driver's Kit:—		
Jackets	..	2	Coats, W.P.	..	1
Pantaloons	.. prs.	1	Gloves, leather	prs.	1
Putties	.. prs.	1	Goggles	prs.	1
Trousers	.. prs.	1			
Waistcoats, cardigan	..	1			
Badges, cap	..	1	Motor Cyclist's Kit:—		
Bags, Kit	..	1	Leggings, leather	prs.	1
Braces	.. prs.	1	Jackets, W.P.	..	1
	clothes	1	Leggings, W.P.	prs.	1
	hair	1	Gloves, leather	prs.	1
Brushes	polish	1	Goggles	prs.	1
	shaving	1			
	tooth	1	Flying Kit:—		
Combs	..	1	Boots, knee or thigh	prs.	1
Forks	..	1	Caps, fur-lined		1
Holdall	..	1	Gauntlets, plain or	prs.	1
Razors	..	1	observers		
Knife, clasp	..	1	Goggles, masks, winter		1
Do. table	..	1	pattern		
Razor	..	1	Goggles, masks, summer		1
Shirts, flannel	..	3	pattern		
Socks, worsted	.. prs.	3	Gloves, triplex, tinted, prs.		1
Spoons	..	1	Do. mackintosh	prs.	1
Towels, hand	..	2	Jackets, leather	..	1
Coats, great	..	1	Overalls, waterproof	prs.	1

(a) See Appendix X, "Instructions regarding Non-Technical Supplies."

CERTIFIED that I have received Kit as detailed on page 2, with the exception of articles noted below.

Station _____

Date _____ *Getchorn*

List of unissued articles—Ordinary Clothing.

(Unused items to be ruled through diagonally.)

Article	No.	Record of subsequent issue		
		Date	Initials of Officer	Initials of man
Brush Brass				
Knife Table				
Ink				
Spoon				

Record of Working Clothing (a).

Issued with combination suits	Yes
Issued with Motor Cyclist Kit	No
Issued with Motor Driver's Kit	No
Issued with Flying Kit	No

(a) "Yes" or "No" to be entered in second column. Record of subsequent issue to be made in third column, where issue is made on enlistment.

Clothing supplied while on the station.

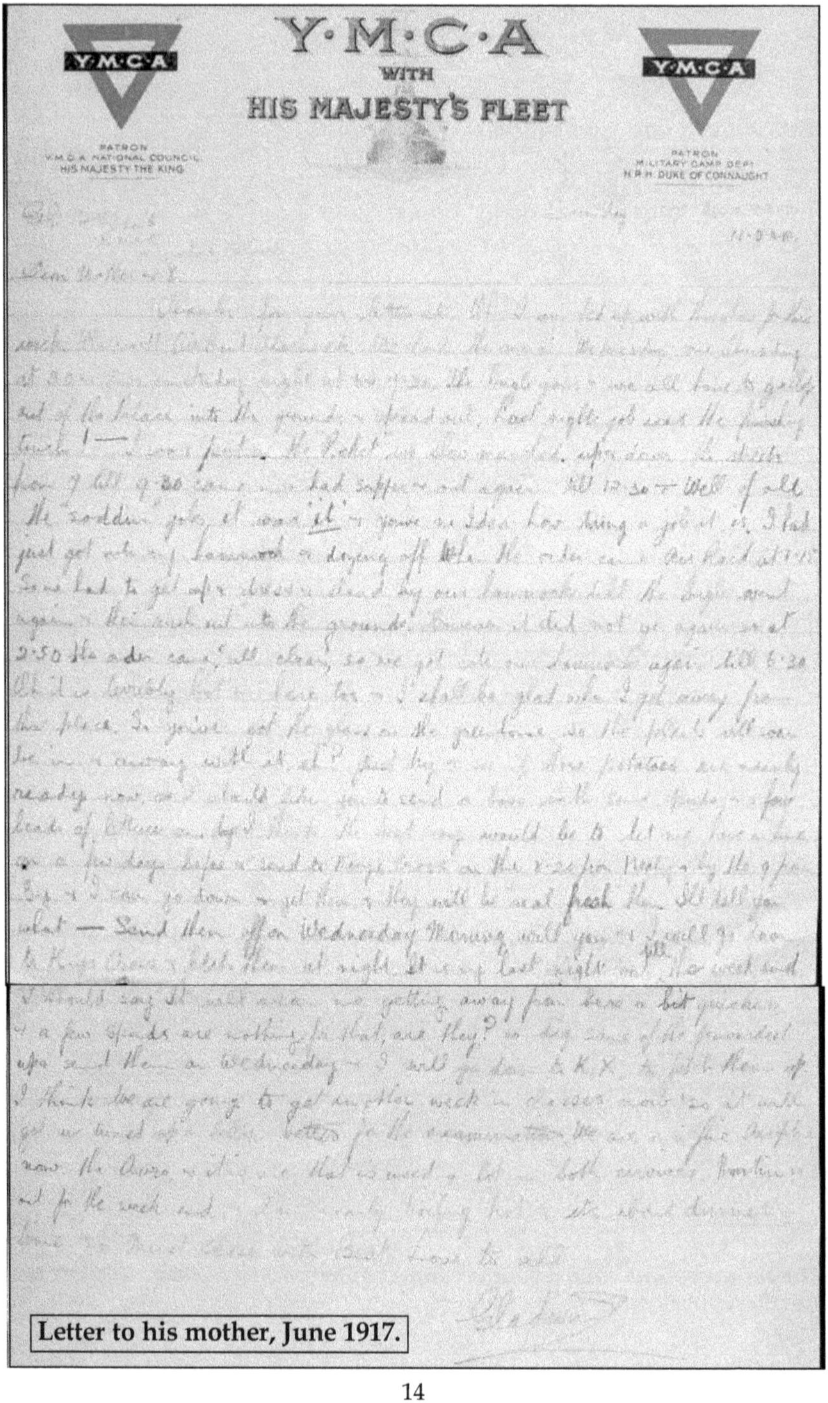

Y·M·C·A

WITH

HIS MAJESTY'S FLEET

Y·M·C·A

PATRON
Y.M.C.A. NATIONAL COUNCIL
HIS MAJESTY THE KING

Y·M·C·A

PATRON
MILITARY CAMP DEPT
H.R.H. DUKE OF CONNAUGHT

[illegible]

Letter to his mother, June 1917.

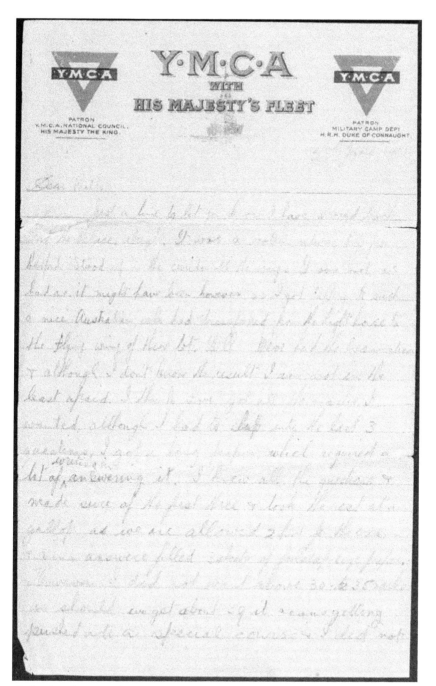

A further letter to his mother in June.

Continuation of his letter.

G.T.W., fourth from right on the back row, peeping through.

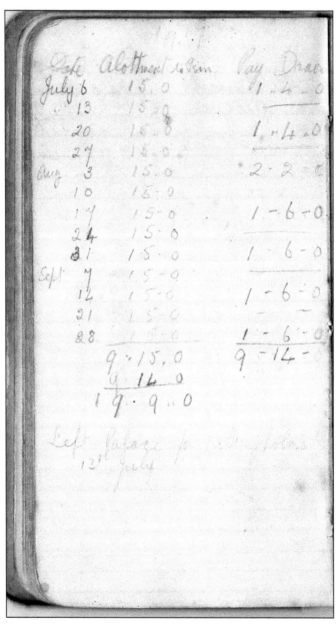

Date	Alottment to Sister	Pay Draw
July 6	15.0	1 . 4 . 0
13	15.0	
20	15.0	1 . 4 . 0
27	15.0	
Aug 3	15.0	2 . 2 . 0
10	15.0	
17	15.0	1 . 6 . 0
24	15.0	
31	15.0	1 . 6 . 0
Sept 7	15.0	
14	15.0	1 . 6 . 0
21	15.0	
28	15.0	1 . 6 . 0
	9 . 15 . 0	9 . 14 .
	9 . 14 . 0	
	19 . 9 . 0	

Left Palace for old follows
13th July

This is an entry from his notebook in 1917, which itemizes his pay, including an allowance for his sister, who was recently widowed with twins to raise. The twins were born in 1916 and their father was killed in action in 1917.

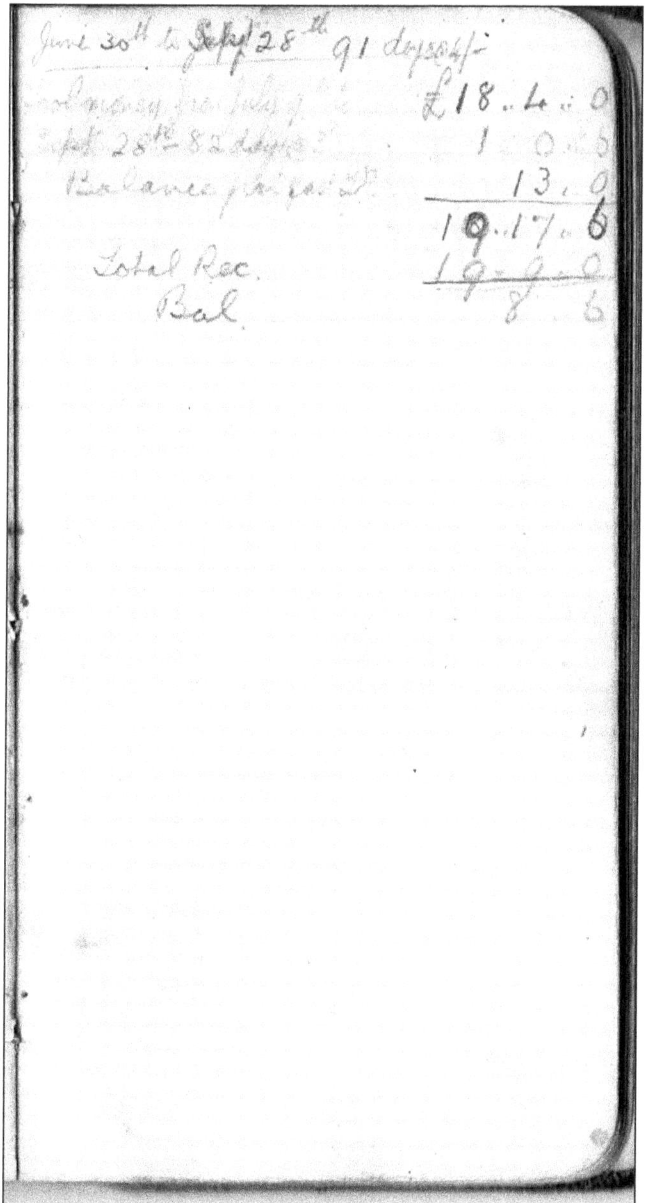

June 30th to Sept 28th 91 days 4/=

tool money from bills of £18..4..0

Sept 28th 82 days 1..0..0

Balance paid forward 13..0

19..17..6

Total Rec. 19..9..0

Bal 8..6

Notebook entry for tool money.

The following pages are printed here from his notebook written while he was training at Crystal Palace.

Parts of an aircraft.

Ailerons

a Balancing flaps: usually hinged to the rear spar of main planes. The movements of which enables the pilot to controll the machine laterally when flying.

'Dihedral'

The ∠ at which main planes are inclined laterally from the horizontal; if upwards it is positive — if downwards it is termed negative.

Incidence

the ∠ at which the planes are set in relation to the line of flight.

Streamline

A Streamline has a gradual change of Curvature along any section, thus eliminating drag or air suction.

Aerofoil

is a structural shape designed to get the maximum amount of lift with a minimum amount of resistance to forward motion.

Parts of an aircraft.

Ribs

... are the light members placed fore & aft in the planes, ... giving them strength & shape to the ...

Stagger

... is the horizontal distance between perpendiculars from the leading edges of the major planes when the machine is at flying level.

Chassis or Undercarriage

The framework on which a machine rests or the structure of a machine, which enables it to run along the ground & to absorb the shock of landing. It includes wheels, skids, & shock absorbers.

Skids

The under members of the undercarriage running fore & aft to which are attached the wheel & axle.

Tail Boom

The tail construction running aft which carries

Parts of an aircraft.

the Empennage &... a Nacelle
type of Machine

Longitudinal Stability
exists when
the longitudinal axis of the
aeroplane... tends to return to
the horizontal.

Lateral Stability
exists when the
transverse axis of the
aeroplane tends to return
to the horizontal.

Flight wires
Run upwards & outwards
bear all strain when machine is in
flight & are usually duplicated.

Landing Wires
Run downwards & outwards
& bear all strain in landing &
when machine is standing.

Parts of an aircraft.

Hints for Men Drafted to a Station.

1) Men should make themselves aquainted with station orders & routine as soon as Possible,

2) Men should make themselves aquainted with all types of machines on the station

3) When effecting a repair, tuneing up or erecting machines the mechanic must always remember that the lives of valuable men/sometimes his own/ depends on his work & that the Pilot looks to him to do his work in a thorough & conscientious manner, he must never scamp his work, & all jobs no matter how small they may be, or seem to be, must be done in a workman like manner, nothing but the best work will do. The omission of a nut, split pin, or a lockingwire; or the failure of a mechanic to detect a frayed control wire, may result in a serious smash.

4) Before reporting a machine ready for flight the mechanic should have a thorough look round, to make sure there are no ends of wire, tools, screws, nuts etc are laying inside the fuselage, nacelle

Rules of the Station.

own planes, as any of these parts
are liable to come in contact with
the working parts of the machine
such as :- propellers, Engine, Controls
etc with very disastrous results.
(5) All materials used on Aeroplane construction are valuable materials & great
care must be taken that the
expenditure is not wasteful.
(6) Remember that the cleanliness of a
machine has a great deal to do with
its efficiency
(7) Many of the important parts on a machine
are difficult to closely examine special
attention should be given to these parts,
as they are easily overlooked & the result
may not be easy to account for.
(8)
Remember that a naked light close
to a machine is a source of danger
both to yourself & to the machine.
If you have any brazing to do
always keep your blow lamp at a
safe distance.
(9) when effecting repairs to a

Rules of the Station and aircraft maintenance.

machine, especially outside when
a Erecting stops, the mechanic is
to hang up a notice on the Engine,
or on some other prominent position.
If this order is not carried out & the
mechanic suddenly called away, the
machine may be taken $\frac{as}{}$
for use & the result may be disaster
[see station notices on this subject]

10)

When told off as deputy carpenter, the mechanic
must always be on the alert, & have a bag
of handy tools to be ready at a moment's
notice. In addition to tools, this ready
use bag should contain sufficient
materials to do small repairs. These
materials should include, an assortment
of small screws, nuts, bolts, adjusters,
copper tacks, ferrules etc. also a small
piece of fabric, & a needle & thread.
If possible the men should obtain
new materials for their ready use
bag. The general rule on most
stations is to provide a larger
ready use box for the use of the
duty Carpenter only. This box

Rules of the Station and aircraft maintenance.

generally contains sufficient materials for repairs on a larger scale. It generally contains wire (both flexible & Piano) ferrules & adjusters of suitable gauges, & an assortment of bolts, nuts, screws, washers, tacks, nails, split pins etc also cord, sandow rubber, fabric dope, acetone, & brushes for using same.

(11) Lubrication of pulleys fairleads etc. All pulleys & fairleads for wires must be lubricated with grease & not with oil.

(12) <u>Bolts & Nuts</u>
             Care must be taken, that when small bolts & nuts are tightened up with a spanner they are not overstrained. If a nut be tightened up too much the bolt will have an initial stress put onto at & the further stress, due to its normal load may be sufficient to cause the bolt to fracture.

Aircraft maintenance.

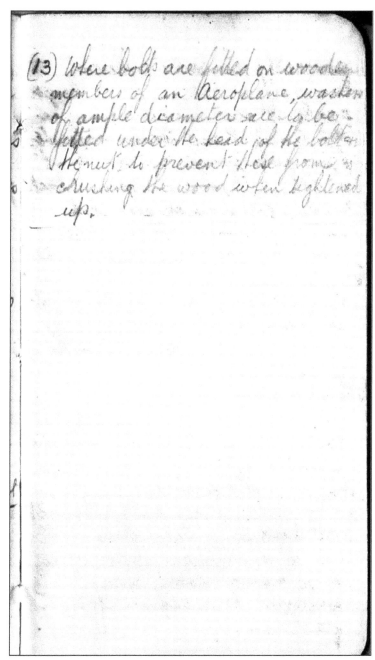

(13) Where bolts are fitted on wooden members of an Aeroplane, washers of ample diameter are to be fitted under the head of the bolt & the nut to prevent these from crushing the wood when tightened up.

Aircraft maintenance.

BE-2C 80 HP R.A.F.

Span 36' 11" Length 27' 0" Gap 6' 3" St[...]

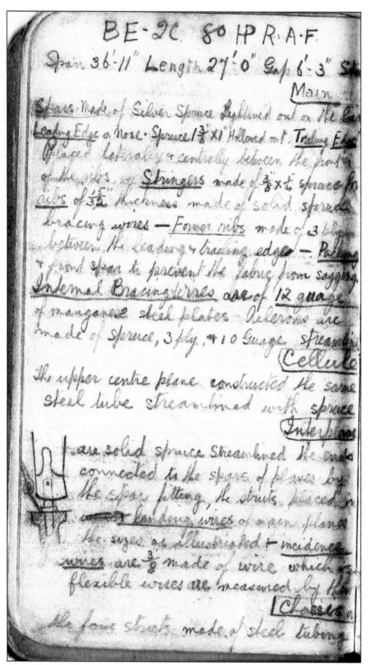

Main

Spars made of Silver Spruce lightened out on the [...]
Leading Edge or Nose. Spruce 1⅜" X 1" Hollowed out. Trailing Edge
[Pl]aced laterally & centrally between the [front]
[spa]rs & ribs use Stringers made of ⅜ x ¼ spruce [for]
ribs of 3/16" thickness made of solid spruce
bracing wires — Former ribs made of 3 ply
between the leading & trailing edge — Pa[cking]
& front spar to prevent the fabric from sagging
Internal Bracing Wires are of 12 gua[ge]
of manganese steel plates. Ailerons are
made of spruce, 3 ply, & 10 Guage stream[line]

Cellule

The upper centre plane constructed the same
steel tube streamlined with spruce

Inter[plane]

[struts] are solid spruce streamlined the ends
connected to the spars of planes by
the spar fitting, the struts placed in
landing wires of main plane
the sizes as illustrated + incidence
wires are ⅜ made of wire which [is]
flexible wires are measured by the

Chassis

the four struts made of steel tubing

Details of planes.

30

2'-0" Dihedral 3½° incidence 3½° Chord 5'-5"
planes.

Principal Dimensions Front Spar 3½" X 1½" Rear ¾ 3
... 5/8 X ¼ - 18 Gauge Streamlined Steel tube ...
... spars - crossing underneath the ...
... purpose of stiffening the ribs — compression
These ribs take the tension of the internal
bracing with ⅛" X 3/16 Spruce flanges fixed
... Former ribs are placed between the leading edge
... between the intermediate ... ribs
... wire connected to the spars by ...
... to rear spars & main ... & are
... tube.

... the main planes the struts are ...
bound with fabric.

Struts
filled with socket made of duralumin
means of an special ... which is part of ...
position as illustrated — The flying
are seven stranded flexible or Cable
... are ⅞ drift wires are ⅜ — controll...
more flexible than the ordinary wire (note)
circumference.

Undercarriage
Streamlined with spruce bound with

Details of planes.

fabric — the Aeroplane wheels attached to a $1\frac{1}{8}''$ steel tube Axle are attached to the undercarriage struts by means of Sandow Elastic rubber. — The bracing rods on the ... of the undercarriage are streamline

FUSELAGE

...made in one, tapering to ½ square at the ... from rear of pilot's seat to the tail. ... the longerons by sockets. Cross Struts ... wires — as the top & bottom of the Fuselage ... tracing wires, the streamline formation ... cockpit is made of 3 ply plane to tail. The whole covered with fabric. The ... either find a thread is turned which enters ... is affected.

Longerons made of ash. Top longerons 4" x $1\frac{1}{8}''$ tapering to
tail — Lower longerons ...
Wing lift Struts are $1\frac{3}{4}''$ x 3" ... spruce connected
$1\frac{3}{4}$ x ½" Spruce held in position by angle
is made of 3 ply, these surfaces have
on top of fuselage from the front to the back & are
by 3 ply bearers 7/2 x ¼" spruce running on
fuselage is braced by strong rods on
a socket by which means adjustment is
Screw

EMPENNAGE.

Details of planes.

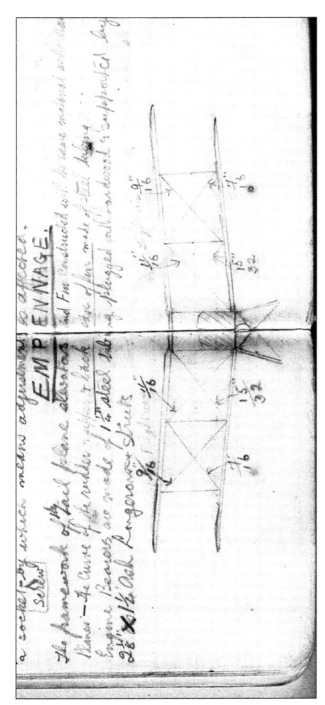

a socket by which means adjustment to aircraft.

[Screw]

EMPENNAGE.

The framework of tail plane elevators Planes — the curve of the rudder ripples & back and Fin constructed will be same material are often made of steel tube & plugged with Engine Bearers are made of 1½" steel tube 2⅛" x 1½" Oak hangerover struts

Details of planes.

Caudron 80 HP Engine

Span upper plane 42'-10½"	Dihedral	NIL
lower " 23'-7"	Stagger	NIL
Length fore aft 23'-3"	incidence	Main Plane
Gap. Between Main 4'-7" Planes	under Nacelle & end strut	
Chord upper plane 5'-3"	Spars level	
" " " 4'-3"	Under intermediate Right Rear	Left Rear
	Spar 12'-10"	Spar 12'-10"
	Above Level	below level

Main Planes. The front Spar (the leading edge of planes) is made of ash bound with tape to give strength, above veneer 6" wide. ... spruce laminations this is Mahogany

The rear Spar. ash, spruce & manganese steel laminations bound with tape. These & us have a knuckle joint on the outside of the intermediate struts for warping the planes. The main planes have warp control & therefore have no ailerons.

RIBS. Light Ribs are made of willow & are very flexible. Compression Ribs are made of solid willow & also 3 ply with spruce flanges.

INTERPLANE STRUTS. Main planes Cellule struts solid ash. Intermediate struts made in three laminations centre of ash & two of spruce. End & also exterior struts are made of two laminations of spruce enclosing steel tube. Extension struts are tension & also compression struts.

Details of planes.

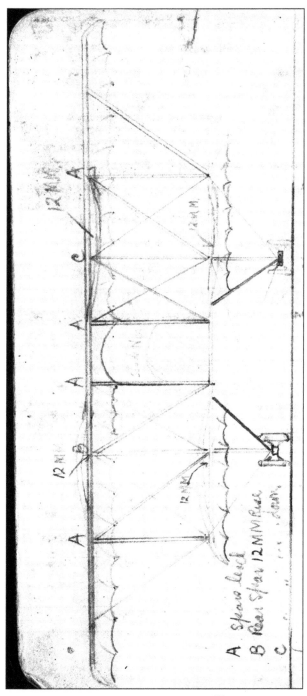

Details of planes.

<u>Seel Diagonal Bracing</u> above Nacelle,

<u>Tail boom a OUT Rigger</u> the top booms are

                         the lower booms a

<u>Tail Boom Struts fa top Booms</u> of spruce

 + bound with tape at measured distan

<u>Empennage Struts</u> made of solid ash.

<u>Tail plane</u> Leading edge made of

           mahogany veneer 6" wide

    "   Ribs etc made of ash a willow.

<u>Nacelle</u> General Construction Longerons a Struts Made of

       The Nacelle contains Pilot y observers seats

       also dural controll columns

<u>Controlls</u>. the warping wires acting as landing y

flying wires on the rear of the main planes

from the intermediate struts outwards.

<u>Empennage Controlls</u>. in previous machines of this

type instead of the usual hinged elevators

as now used, a part of the tail plane was

flexible being controlled as a warping plane

<u>Rudder</u> Controlls connected to foot bar.

<u>Elevator</u>   "   "   " Controll Column

Details of planes.

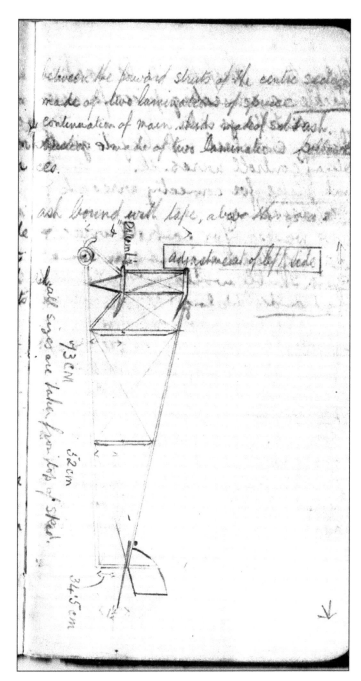

Details of planes.

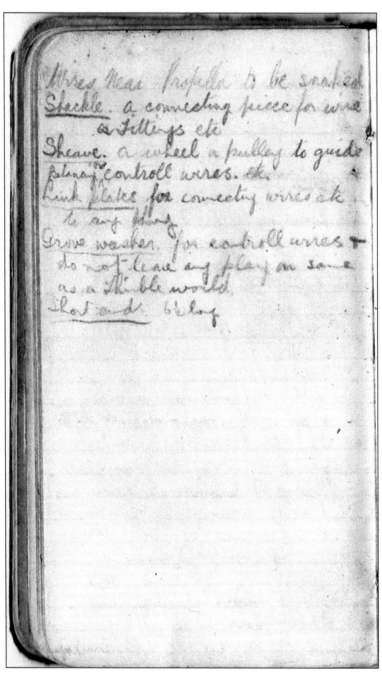

Wires near Propellor to be snaked
Shackle. a connecting piece for wire
        & fittings etc
Sheave. a wheel a pulley to guide
pulley, controll wires. etc.
Link plates for connecting wires etc
        to any thing
Grove washer. for controll wires &
do not leave any play on same
as a thimble would.
Slot end below

Details of planes.

38

Erecting & Trueing up.

Curbs Trueing up Fuselage, Longeron
& Compression Struts, spruce)
first 5 bays are turn, wires. other bays
Piano wires. all turnbuckle adjustment
Tail plane ~~~~~~~~ fixed non lifting tail
plane, Drift or Stabilizing Fin, plumb.
Top Longeron is dead level in flight
also (Engine bearers, which are always on
any machine when trued up)
Front Compression strut 1/4 down

$$1° = 1'' \text{ in } 4 ft \ 9\frac{1}{2}$$

At level ... ... made ... ...
by 4ft 9½ & that more, height in inches
above cellule strut top of straight line
string from wing tip to ...
Machine flying. tail heavy decrease
stagger or increase incidence on
tail plane, working tail plane. if it
is not a fixed one
increase of incidence is wash in
de ... ... out.
wing flying down increase incidence
on flat plane.
To fix planes square with fuselage

Erecting and trueing up.

39

trammel from centre of rudder
post to end strut fitting.

air screw Tractor
Propellor Pusher
                Trueing up main plane

landing drift wires

flight drift wires

Plane Bspars, leading edge,
    trailing edge.
    Compression Strut
    Box Rib
    Compression Rib
    Former Rib

level 3 stools always
nail uprights a ___ at all
compression Ribs. Strug line.
Square first bay near roots

Erecting and trueing up.

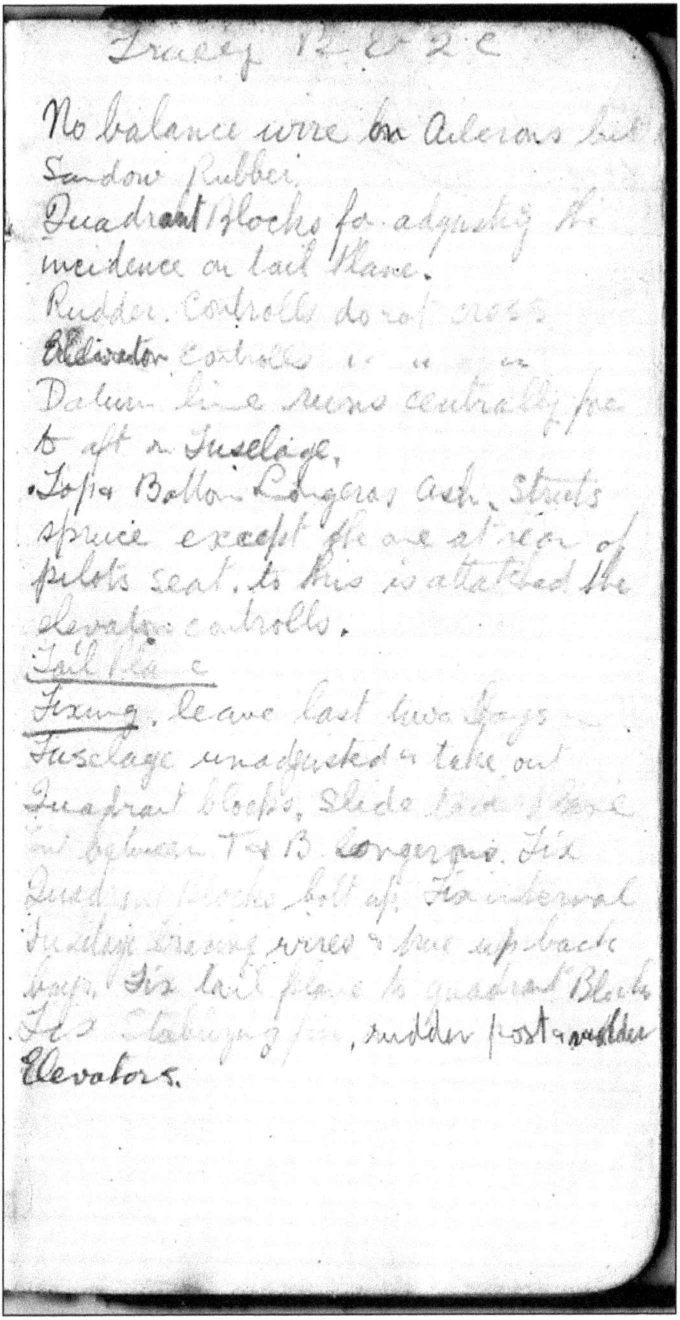

Tracey B.E.2.c

No balance wire on Ailerons but
Sandow Rubber.
Quadrant Blocks for adjusting the
incidence on tail plane.
Rudder. Controlls do not cross
Elevator controlls " " " "
Datum line runs centrally fore
to aft on Fuselage.
Top & Bottom Longerons ash. Struts
spruce except the one at rear of
pilots seat, to this is attached the
elevator controlls.
Tail Plane
Fixing, leave last two Bays
Fuselage unadjusted & take out
Quadrant blocks. Slide tail plane
out between T & B. Longerons. Fix
Quadrant Blocks bolt up. Fix internal
Fuselage bracing wires & true up back
bays. Fix tail plane to quadrant Blocks
Fix Stabilizing fin, rudder post & rudder
Elevators.

Erecting and trueing up.

41

3% Bristol Scout

Dihedral $1\frac{3}{4}°$ incidence $1·8"$

Stagger $16\frac{1}{2}$.

Top longeron level = Flying level,

No Stabilizing Fin, Aileron Controlls

run inside planes.

Timbers Silver Spruce. Leading Edge

& Trailing edge Manganese steel.

Adjustable tail plane.

Front of longerons, Ash.

Chassis, 2 ash & 2 spruce Struts bound with

fabric or Egyptian tape.

Packing for Road transport

Tie Tie bar firmly underneath fuselage

under Cellule +, strut to Rear,

Pack all rough fittings with packing

or felt, Pack packing on leading edge

on timbers at side of fuselage. After

wrapping up & packing, all fittings on

Empennage, tail planes, elevator, Rudders

Specifications for repair of a Bristol Scout.

Avro 80 HP Gnome

Stagger 2ft. Incidence 4°
Dihedral 3° Tail Plane Incidence 4°
Ash Longerons, Silver Spruce
compression Struts.
Centre Cellule Struts. Ash.
Main Skid & tail Skid Ash.
flying level is top longeron
for pilots seat to front.
Datum line. centre of strut
at rear of pilots seat & centre of
strut of rear of machine. and
1ft 6½ from top of top longeron
at front of pilots seat & front.
Main Planes. wash in of ½" on
outer rear Strut.
Aileron Controlls. 2 balance wires
& 2 distance wires. & 2 douhroll
wires.
Centre Cellule struts Plumb.
Tail Plane fastened to top
longeron.
Engine shaft 1' 3½" below top of longeron
Therefore datum line is 3" lower = 1'6½"
Dihedral is set by setting staff.
Trueing up fuselage sides top
taper bottom together

undercarriage. Fix Steel struts to
skid & wheel for axle
<u>Tail Unit erection.</u>

Fix tube on rear of drift fin through
hole in rear of fuselage. Fix tail
plane in holes in fuselage at
leading edge, connect adjustment
wires between Stabilizing fin & tail
plane & lower longerons & tail plane
True tail plane by holding straight edge
under fuselage & take leading edge
out of winding with straight edge
Fix Rudder to Rudder post & Elevators
to Tail Plane.

(Also seeing Stabilizing fin is plumbed)

Connect rudder & Elevator Controls.
Plumb centre cellule struts in each
direction by cellule bracing wires.
Box planes & fix. Set Dihedral
by. Dihedral trammel lath. Set
by nominal leading Edge

6"/2⅝ 6"2⅝ 8'3¾ 8'3¾ ½" ½" with Trailing Edge

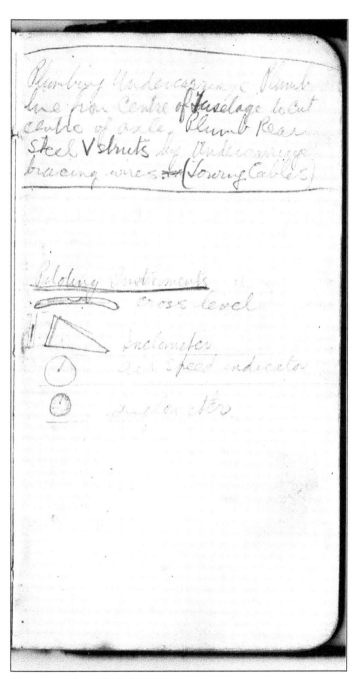

Plumbing Undercarriage Plumb
line from Centre of Fuselage to Cut
centre of axle. Plumb Rear
Steel V struts by Undercarriage
bracing wires. (Towing Cables)

Piloting Instruments

Cross level

Inclinometer

air speed indicator

inclinometer

Avro 80, also pilot's instruments.

45

White Tractor Seaplane &
(225 H Sunbeam.)

Top longeron flying level
Turnbuckle adjustment. Cable wires to
hay at rear of Pilot seat, remainder
Main & Longerons spruce. comp. Strut
spruce. Engine bearers solid Spruce.
Chassis Steel tubes streamlined
with Fairing bound with fabric.
Planes double camber. hinged
to Cellule ⌒⌒ solid Spruce Spar
L Edge Spruce hollowed out C
9 interplane Struts. in each box
4 solid. 5 hollowed out two lamination
Spruce a bound with fabric at measured
distances. Top plane has a indentation
over bottom, planes. Ailerons wider &
have no balance wires
Empanage
            Fixed slightly lighter lifting
tail plane. 2 drift pins T for Bottom

Specifications for repair of White Tractor Seaplane with a
225-horsepower Sunbeam engine.

Sheer legs

Height = 3 times foot span. ...
bending Chain with Timber hitch +
11 turns + 10 riding turns + finish up
with clove hitch. When a lean to
fitted with block = 'Purchase' ...
Drop round +

Propeller Torque

Tendency of propeller to throw
machine in the opposite direction
to what the propeller is revolving.

Pitch of Propeller

is the distance the propeller
travels in one revolution in a
... density of air.

Specifications for repair of White Tractor Seaplane with
a 225-horsepower Sunbeam engine.

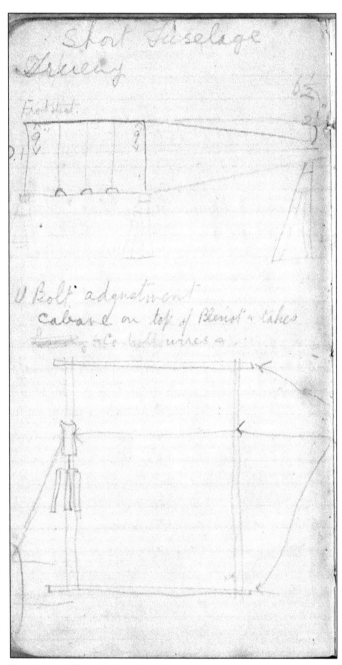

Trueing a Short plane fuselage. .

Bleriot Tractor Monoplane

Main plane :- Warp Controll.

~~~~ .... Dihedral ....

L, 9 Fixed wires

4 wires are attached to the Cabane

F....... .... Turnbuckle adjustment att. to
Cabane

Rear L. wires Passed through sleeves
on Cabane & act as Balancing ......

Flying Wires

2 front Flying wires att. to chassis ....
....

2 Rear fly-wires are attached to
Pylon & act as controll wires.

Undercarriage
upper & lower Banches,
connected .... by two standards
struts V sold ......
.... are .... Rubber
att. to sliding collar round standard
to this collar are steel rods which
..... to wheel axle kept in position
by radius rods ..... between wheels
distance rod. .... undercarriage check
wires are ....
rubber to ....

Bleriot Tractor Monoplane.

49

Trueing up Bleriot

Planches must be level, & centre
of fuselage centre of planches.

Tail Plane. Bolted to
bottom longerons on pivot
& two steel adjustable quadrants
at rear of tail plane
2 adjustable v shaped steel tubes
stays to level tail plane.
Elevator partially balanced rudder
no drift fin partially balanced rudder

True up fuselage
Strut in rear of Pilots seat
forward the bottom longerons
flying level remainder of machine
is symetrical. U bolt adjustment
each one trued up separately
incidence 7⅛°
Dihedral 1 in 25 or 6%
Main Plane Front & Rear
spars range of spruce tube as
uprights, ribs laced, leading edge
oregon pine. Wing tips ash

Trueing a Bleriot Tractor Monoplane.
50

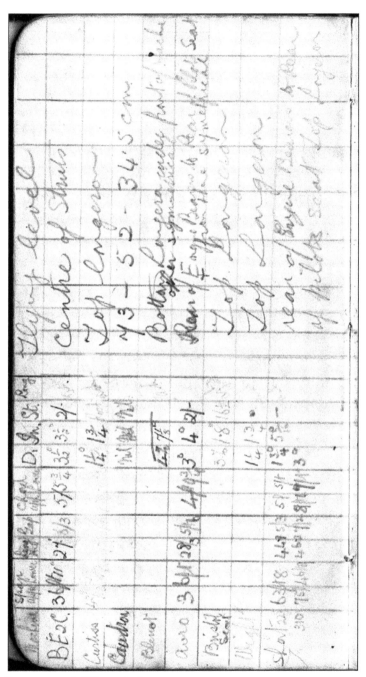

Summary of different planes.

Caudron

All Controlls Cable wires
remander Piano
Warping Controll wires act as
Flying Wires.
Balance Wires act as landing wires
~~to wires~~ extra tip plane
adjustable left plane by lindard
To assemble
4 Trestles levelled all ways.
2 under Nacelle + 2 under end and out
Struts to catch both Spars.
Box up planes & lift on Trestles.
Use undercarriage as undercarriage
bolt go through Spars. Put in
nacelle everything in all in Nacelle
Nacelle as landing Stag. Dihedral
level through front Spar. Propellor
Torque now to counteract ... give
Right Rear Spar 12 m.m above level
on intermediate strut & Left rear
Spar 12.m.m below level at intermediate
strut. that is wash out on R.H. spar
Set clock at neutral & tighten up every
Controll wires. Sweep up Planes
with rear spar by way of wash
so out the rear struts have

Details of a Caudron seaplane.

52

a 24 m.m. difference in height.
plumb struts by bearing through
inter plane strut. Wheels att to struts
by Radius Rods + Sandow Rubber.
Erect Tail plane is main plane.
erect Drift fin strut & guide struts
plumb. & guide struts. Trammel
centre bay between Drift fin.
Erect Tail Booms. att. tail
planes to booms. by Traadrow + bolts
at rear. Trueing up the whole
Left hand side only.
Work point of centre on strut's
measure 73 c.m. 52 - + 34.5 cm
ship line & set to flying level.
next level through Tail Plane
on leading edge to take two
bottom Booms out of winding
Take whole boom out of square by
stay wires

Details of a Caudron seaplane.

Sopwith Schneider (Pup)

Front Struts 4ft 4½
Rear " 4ft 5¼
Span 25ft 8" Chord 5'-2"
Length Fore + aft 20ft
Incidence main planes 2°
Tail plane 1" + to width
Dihedral 2·4° or 1in 21·5
Stagger 8" Flying level Top longeron

_____

310 HP Short

Span 74'-6" folded 20'-9
Chord 6ft 11" gap 6ft 11"
Length overall 18'-6"
" " 17'-4"
Incidence 5° Dihedral 5°
Weight unloaded 4,033 lbs
loaded 7,014
Speed at 2000 feet 63 knots
climb 2,000 feet in 12 minutes
5,000 " 53½ "

Measurements of Sopwith Schneider (Pup) and 310hp Short.

Baby S. S.

Spa 5 to feet (top flap
40 feet (lower flap)
Stop 5 ft 3 c nd 5 ft
Deflection rel, stagger nil
incidence 5° tail plane run 3°
Aileron 15 ft 3 long g i ft 8 to 2 ft 8
Balsflap float, 3 incidence)

22 5 Short

Incidence 5° Dihedral 7 or 3 3
Span 63 ft 3 9 ft 5 ft
Lead 5 ft stagger nil
Bows of float 29 tail plane 2°

Measurements of Baby Short and 225 Short.

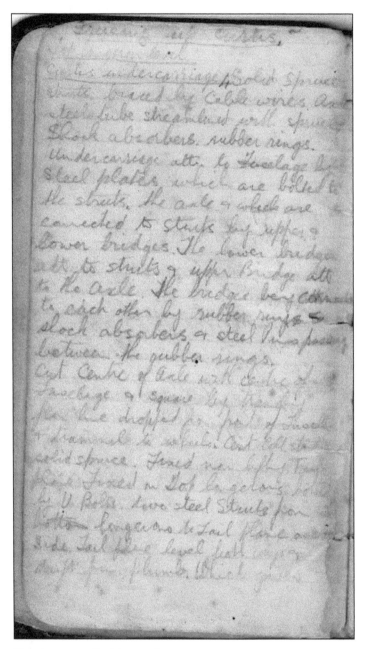

Trueing up a Curtis seaplane.

First two bayrows from... ...one aileron... top flanch only... top flange... 10" ... 1½" incidence to... Steel Struts... ... cellule. ...

B E 2 C

Long ash Struts spruce...
Swage rods. ...
Steel Strut...
Experimental Skid...
...solid ash ... **6** solid ash Struts...
axle steel ... wood...
Erecting.

axle connected to ... by
...rubber shock absorbers...
struts with sockets, + brace...
...principle by cable wires.
Set 2 ... parallel by distance...
cut centre of distance rods centre of...
Centre of Fuselage.

Trueing up a Curtis seaplane.

4. Starting at Killingholme

On 13th July 1917, G.T.W. was posted to the air station at Killingholme, North Lincolnshire.

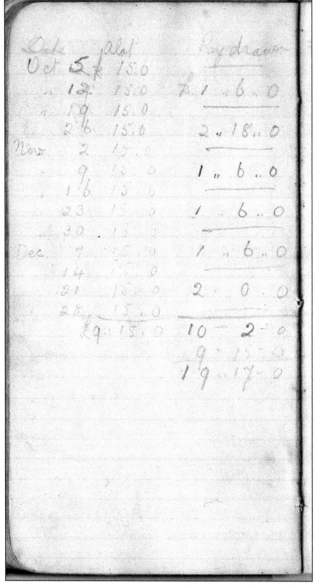

Pay from 5th October 1917 to 28th December 1917.

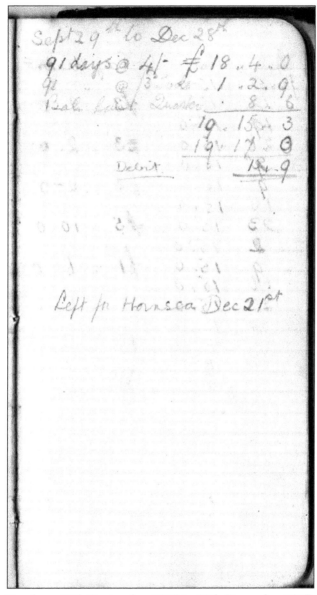

Sept 29th to Dec 28th

91 days @ 4/- £ 18 . 4 . 0

91 @ 3 1 . 2 . 9

Bal. Last Quarter 8 . 6

19 . 15 . 3

19 . 17 . 0

Debit 1 . 9

Left for Hornsea Dec 21st

Pay from 29th September 1917 to 28th December 1917.

59

TO BE HANDED TO BOOKING CLERK.

Wt. 14710/M81. 150,000. 1/16.
(50,000). J. P. & Co., Ltd.

Forms
O. 1800.
T.

Army Form O. 1800.
(In Pads of 50.)

No.

APPLICATION for issue of Third-Class Railway Tickets at reduced fares to **MEN** of His Majesty's Forces, Naval and Military (including Territorials and National Reservists), and of Ambulance Corps engaged with the Forces proceeding on leave.

_____

Fare to be paid at time of booking.

To the Booking Clerk at _Killingholme_
(any Railway Station in Great Britain and Ireland).

Please issue to bearer, in uniform,. a Third-Class Return Ticket to _Grimsby_ *Station, on payment of the Single Fare for the Return journey, and on surrender of this Voucher.

_____   _____
                                                        Signature of Officer Commanding.

To be filled in by Booking Clerk.

No. of Ticket Issued.   Fare Paid.   Initials of Booking Clerk.

Unless this Voucher is surrendered at the time of booking, the ordinary fare will be chargeable, and no refund will be made in respect of the extra fare or fares paid.

*If the Booking Clerk cannot issue a Ticket through to destination, he will book to furthest point and issue a re-booking Voucher.

Railway Pass from Killingholme to Grimsby.

Killingholme flyingboat on the river Humber, 1918/19

'K' Top of Slipway. F. Boat.

"K" F. Boat 1918-19

"K" Motor Launch + F. Boat

"K" - Shipway 225 Short 1917-18

F. Boat 1918-19

K. 1919 D.H.6

'K' Sopwith Schneider
1918-19.

"K" "225" Short 1917

Concrete "K" 1917

The R.N.A.S. leaves Killingholme to go to Hornsea. The American flag is being raised at Killingholme as the Americans took over.

5. Move to Hornsea Mere

G.T.W. moved from Killingholme to Hornsea Mere on 21st December 1918 and was billed in what is now the ex-servicemen's club at Back Southgate, Hornsea.

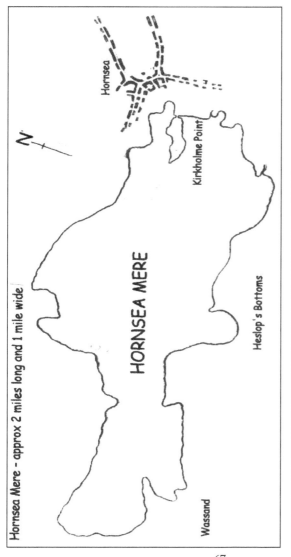

Civilian use. Shows Hornsea Mere pre-war activities.

Hornsea Mere - approx 2 miles long and 1 mile wide

N

Hornsea

Kirkholme Point

HORNSEA MERE

Heslop's Bottoms

Wassand

JAMES T. HOLMES,
BOAT BUILDER, &c.,
HORNSEA MERE.

All kinds of Boats Built to Order.
Repairs neatly executed.

PLEASURE BOATS ON HIRE, One Shilling per hour.

A LAWN TENNIS COURT near the Boathouse.—Season Tickets, 10s. 6d.; Monthly, 5s.; or Four Players, 3d. per hour each; Three Players, 4d. per hour each; Two Players, 6d. per hour each.

REFRESHMENTS.—Hay's Lemonade, Ginger Ale, and Ginger Champagne; Carter's Lemonade, Ginger Beer, and Soda Water. Farrah's original Harrogate Toffee.

67

The road to the station at Kirkholme Point.

Kirkholme Point today.

The original fire bell of the station, made from a reject cylinder from an aircraft engine.

Guard Room Hornsea

On entering the station was the guard room, which later became the R.S.P.B. bird lookout until 1999.

Camp Hornsea 1918

Bessoneau Hangars.

Flying coat
displayed in
Hornsea Museum.

The same view today of where the Bessaneau Hangars were.

The only form of communication the plane had, once in the air, were the two pigeons they had placed in a pocket. In case of emergency, they wrote a message on small piece of paper which was rolled up and put in a small tube on the pigeon's leg. The pigeon was released from the plane.

Pigeons were noted for their speed at delivering messages, which was up to 60mph.

Pigeon Loft. Hornsea 1918.

Mere Compass Adjusting Platform today. This was the circle that planes were put on to adjust their compasses as there was no magnetic pull

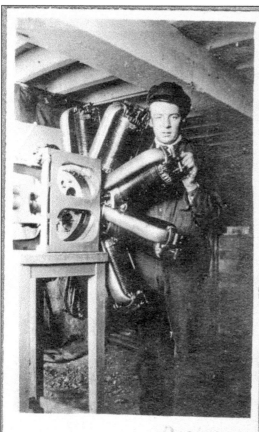

The shed between the café and the Mere existing today was used as a 'dope house.' This is where the wings were painted with a liquid to tighten the canvass cloth which covered the wings. The liquid was hallucinogenic. Men working here were allowed to work for only half an hour without a break and then were made to drink a pint of milk and go for a one-mile walk for fresh air.

Dickie

Workshop, currently being used as a café.

The above building was erected as a generator house but not used. It was also a temporary mortuary in case of multiple fatalities.

Hornsea Slipway

The Mere south of Kirkholme Point.

The same view today.

"Coming In"

The same view today.

Tweenie.   Tempo.   Wag.

Hornsea.   Schneider. 1918

Tommy. War + Paul.

Lock & Braz

"Dickie"

Nich & Lock.

Hornsea Aug - 1918   Jock - B. Nick - Over. 1918
HORNSEA

A Little Game

Some of the personnel photographed in the early days.

81

Lill -Tweenie -Mabs -Dick -Dick- War -Nickie

Some more of the personnel photographed in the early days.

Lill - Cam - Smith

Airships were often seen flying over the station.

Flying over the Bessoneau Hanger.

NS 8. Hornsea

6. Working on the Station

G.T.W.'s notebook entries.

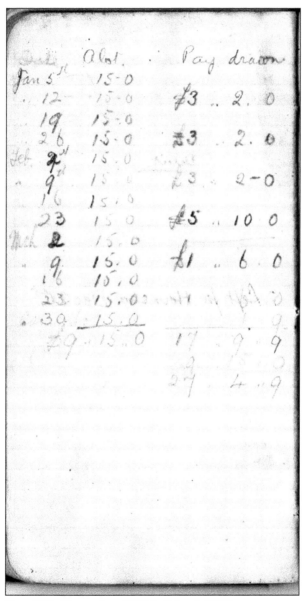

Pay, 29th December 1917 to March 1918.

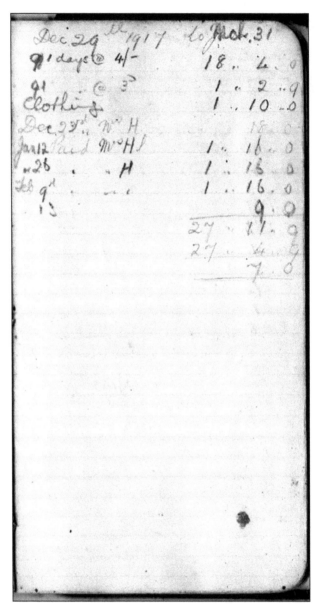

Dec 29th 1917 to March 31		
91 days @ 4/-	18 .. 4 .. 0
91 @ 3d	1 .. 2 .. 9
Clothing	1 .. 10 .. 0
Dec 29d W H	18 .. 0
Jan 12 paid MrsH	1 .. 16 .. 0
" 26 " " H	1 .. 16 .. 0
Feb 9d	1 .. 16 .. 0
13	9 .. 0
	27 .. 17 .. 9
	27 9
	7 .. 0

Pay, 29th December 1917 to March 1918.

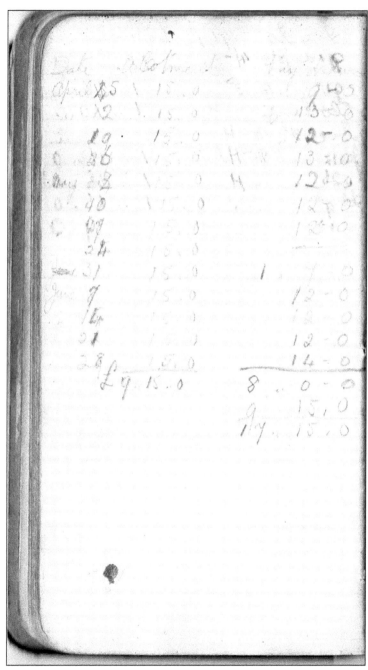

Pay, April to June 1918.

April 1st to June 30th

91 days @ 4d = £18 4 . 0
Brot for   7 . 0
                   18 . 11 . 0
                   17 . 15 . 0
                    . 16 . 0

Pay, April to June 1918.

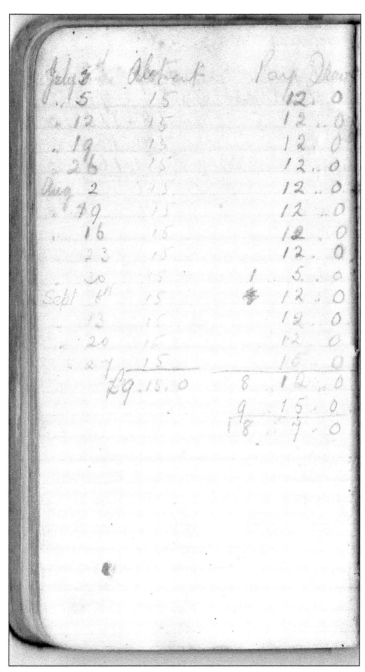

July 5	Abatement	Pay Drawn
" 5	15	12 . 0
" 12	15	12 .. 0
" 19	15	12 . 0
" 26	15	12 .. 0
Aug 2	15	12 .. 0
" 19	15	12 .. 0
16	15	12 . 0
23	15	12 . 0
30	15	1 .. 5 .. 0
Sept 1st	15	12 . 0
13	15	12 .. 0
20	15	12 . 0
27	15	16 . 0
£9 .15. 0	8 .. 14 .. 0
	9 . 15 . 0
	18 .. 7 . 0

Pay, July to Sept 1918.

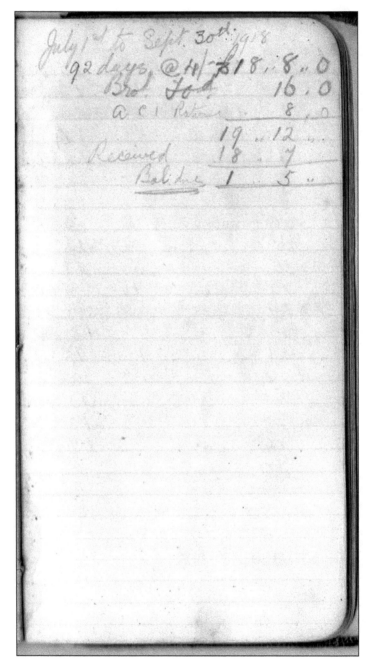

July 1st to Sept. 30th 1918
92 days @ 4/- £18..8..0
Bro. Ford   16.0
@ 6.1 Ration   8..0
                 19..12..
Received   18..7
Balance   1..5..

Pay, July to Sept 1918.

	alot	Pay draw
Oct 5th	15. 0	18. 0
„ 11	15. 0	12. 0
„ 18	15. 0	12. 0
„ 25	15. 0	14 0
Nov 1	15. 0	12. 0
„ 7		12. 0
„ 14		12. 0
„ 29th	2 -	0. 0
Dec 6th		12. 0
„ 16th	5 -	17. 0
„ 23d Rahma	1 -	5. 0
1919		
Jan 10		12. 0
„ 16	1	4. 0
„ 24		12. 0
„ 31		13. 0
Feb 7		13. 0
„ 14		17. 0
„ 20	8	2. 2

alotmts

if drawn till 20th		26 „ 19 „ 2
March 25		18 „ 15. 0
25 weeks @ 15/- 18.15.0	45 „ 14 „ 2

Pay, October to January 1919.

91

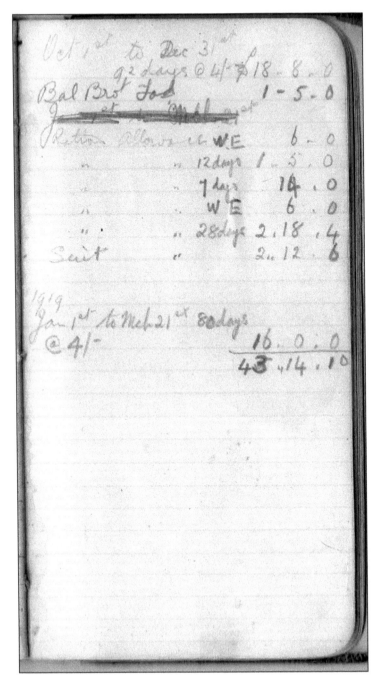

Oct 1st to Dec 31st
    92 days @ 4/- £18 . 8 . 0
Bal Brot Ford   1 - 5 - 0

Ration Allowce ʺ W E   6 - 0
    ʺ   ʺ 12 days 1 . 5 . 0
    ʺ   ʺ 7 days   14 . 0
    ʺ   ʺ   W E   6 . 0
    ʺ   ʺ 28 days 2 . 18 . 4
Suit   ʺ   2 . 12 . 6

1919
Jan 1st to Meh 21st 80 days
    @ 4/-   16 . 0 . 0
                        43 . 14 . 10

Pay, October to January 1919.

92

The duty of the airmen was to keep the planes in good repair so that a dawn and dusk patrol could be kept. This meant flying Hornsea to Flamborough Head, and down to Spurn Point and back to Hornsea. They were mainly looking for German U-Boats.

A concrete slipway was put in at South Landing, Flamborough, should the R.N.A.S. need to beach.

Apart from working on the aircraft, the personnel had to take it in turns on guard duty. This could be quite frightening as there were no lights as they marched around the station and the roadway, and they could easily stand on the local wildfowl. The men added to their diet by collecting duck and wildfowl eggs, which were abundant on the Mere. They ate them for breakfast.

One of the guards was with one of the local girls and the fog came down. When the next guard took over, he wasn't to be found. Afterwards they agreed on a special hook in a tree to hang their rifle on to let the others know they had gone off with a girl. The R.N.A.S. was known locally as the Rather Naughty After Sunset Brigade.

One windy night, G.T.W. was on guard duty. Among the planes, he heard a cracking noise and there were two big eyes looking at him. As he was wondering what to do, there was another crack and the eyes disappeared. This happened another once or twice when he realized one of the canvas covers had come loose and he was looking at the new luminous night-flying dials of the plane.

G.T.W. was on guard duty very late one night and he heard a splashing and loud rumbling noise in the reeds to the north-east of the guard room. He moved towards the noise and, as he had been instructed how to challenge but had never had the chance to do it before, he moved forward with his unloaded rifle. He had no ammunition and said firmly: "Halt, who goes there?" A small voice replied: "It's only me Mr. Gelsthorpe; it's George Veaney." G.T.W., recognizing the voice of young George, who was one of his Sea Cadets, asked what he was doing. "Stealing cans of petrol," came the reply. The Veaneys ran the Victoria Hotel. They were the first people in Hornsea to have a motor taxi and as petrol was scarce they had to steal it to keep the taxi service going. G.T.W. helped young George to carry the petrol home and had a pint of ale before returning back to guard duty.

During the day, when jobs and duties were completed, men would make items of wood and sell them round the town.

The pilot, Flight Lieutenant H. C. Lemon, and his observer, Paul Robertson, took off from Hornsea Mere fully loaded with heavy bombs and ammunition and, having gained a little height, tried turning without ailerons. He slid sideways and crashed into Heslop's Bottoms (see map) and immediately burst into flames. Pilot Officer Lemon was killed but his observer escaped with bad burns.

Flight Commander Paul Robertson was presented with the Albert Medal, later exchanged for a George Cross.

Cigarette box made with the tunic buttons of pilot Flt. Lt. H. C. Lemon on the front.

Part of a propeller made from laminated mahogany.

Propeller boss made into a fruit bowl.

Suitcase made from packing crates from the Sopwith Aviation Co.

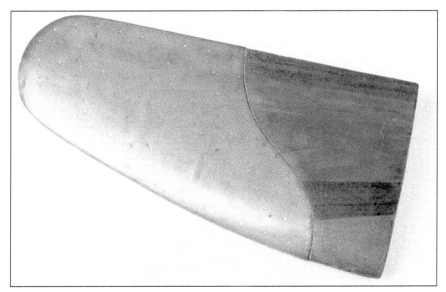

A mahogany propeller tip sheaved in brass plate.

One day, the Mere was iced over as it usually was in the early part of the twentieth century. Young Freddy Medley went out skating on the Mere and went through the ice. Personnel of the R.N.A.S. saw it happen, immediately going to Harker's Farm to get some long stack ladders. They skated across the ice and pulled the lad out. Freddy Medley later became a hairdresser in Newbegin.

One C.O., who was a pilot officer, stopped all the spare-time work of the men and gave them menial tasks, which was not liked. He had to go. The engineers worked out how long it took to drain a seaplane's oil tank and what size hole had to be drilled in the oil tank so the plane would ditch well out to sea. When the C.O. was going up to pilot a patrol, the matchstick which had been placed in the drilled hole to stop it leaking, was taken out before take-off; and the plane did not come back on time. It had obviously ditched.

The next morning the C.O. was back on duty.

"What happened, Sir?" asked the men.

"The old kite seized up well out to sea. Fortunately there was a Grimsby trawler nearby and I took the seaplane down alongside and they brought me back to Grimsby and I got the train back to be on duty now."

Spanish flu broke out while Hornsea Mere was an R.N.A.S. Station and around twelve personnel died of it.

7. Closedown of the station

In the *The Times* of 13th December 1919 and 16th December 1919, The Disposal Board of Munitions were advertising Hornsea Mere for sale. Lady Strickland Constable wrote to the paper to say that it was her property, not the ministry's, and they had no right to sell it.

The civic dignitaries discussed a memorial for the men who lost their lives during the war and it was decided to build a cottage hospital.

The cottage hospital.

8. Back to Civilian Life

Form Z. 518.

CERTIFICATE OF EMPLOYMENT DURING THE WAR.

(To be completed for and handed to each airman.)

Every airman is advised to send a copy, rather than the original, when corresponding with a prospective employer.

It is particularly important that an apprentice whose apprenticeship has been interrupted by military service should have recorded on this Form any employment in a trade similar to his own in which he has been engaged during such military service.

No. *223642*

Rank *1st a.m.*

Names in full (surname first) *GELASTHORPE GLADWIN WEBSTER THOMAS*

Unit *348 Squadron* R.A.F. Trade *Carpenter*

1. Employment in the R.A.F., R.N.A.S., or R.F.C.

	Trade.		Period.	
(a)	*CARPENTER (RNAS)*	From *24/2/17*	To *31/3/18*
(b)	*Do (RAF)*	„ *1/4/18*	„ *Feb./19*
(c)	....	„	„ ....

Employment in any unit of the Naval or Military Forces of the Crown.

	Trade.		Period.	
(a)	....	From	To ....
(b)	....			

If an airman has re-mustered in the course of his service in the R.N.A.S., R.F.C. or R.A.F., the period of his working at each trade should be given.

2. Trade or calling before enlistment (as shown in A.B. 64).

   Joiner + builder

3. (i) Courses of Instruction in the R.A.F., R.N.A.S. or R.F.C., and certificates, if any.

   (a) *6 weeks General Course of Rigging at ...*

   (b) ....

   (c) ....

   (ii) Courses of Instruction in the R.N.; and certificates, if any.

   (a) ....

   (b) ....

   (iii) Army Courses of Instruction and Courses in Active Service Army Schools.

   (a) ....

   (b) ....

G.T.W.'s Employment Certificate.

99

4. R.A.F. qualifications as shown in F.S. Form 280.

Degree of proficiency Satisfactory

5. Special remarks as to qualifications or work done during employment with reference to above.

Character very good.

Signature of airman
(for identification purposes).   Signed...*G. Edwd Mayes*...........................

(Rank)........*L.A.C.*...........

...........................*Capt.*...Commanding...*218 Sqdn.*......... (Unit)

OFFICE STAMP.

___

Notes.—The object of this certificate is to assist the airman in obtaining employment on his return to civil life. The Form will be completed as soon as possible in accordance with Demobilisation Regulations, R.A.F. para. 1109.

As soon as signed and completed it will be given to the airman concerned and will remain his property. He should receive it as early as is compatible with making the necessary references, in order that he can either send it home or keep it in his possession.

One Form will be issued to each man and no duplicate can ever be issued.

(206) WL55042/2079 12/18 600m (16) D.St.

PROTECTION CERTIFICATE AND CERTIFICATE OF IDENTITY

(SOLDIER NOT REMAINING WITH THE COLOURS).

Dispersal Unit Stamp and date of dispersal.

Surname *GELSTHORPE*
(Block letters)

Christian Names *GLADWIN WEBSTER THOMAS*

Regtl. No. *227050*   Rank *Pte*   Record Office *Prb*

Unit _____   Regt. or *R.A.F.*   Pay Office *Woking*
                Corps

I have received an advance of £2.   † Address for Pay *5 Abbey Drive W*

(Signature of Soldier) *G W Gelsthorpe*   *Grimsby*

The above-named soldier is granted 28 days' furlough   Theatre of War or } *N.E. area*
                                                              Command

from the date stamped hereon pending   (as far   Born in the Year *1890*

as can be ascertained) which will date from the last day   Medical Category *B*

of furlough after which date uniform will not be worn   Place of rejoining in }
                                                              case of emergency }

except upon occasions authorised by Army Orders.   Specialist Military }
                                                          Qualification }
      * If for Final Demobilisation insert 1.
        Demobilisation insert 2.
        Transfer to Reserve insert 3.

† As this is the address to which pay and discharge documents will be sent unless further notification is received, any change of address must be reported at once to the Record Office and the Pay Office as noted above, otherwise delay in settlement will occur.

This Certificate must be produced when applying for an Unemployed Sailor's and Soldier's Donation Policy or, if demanded, whenever applying for Unemployment benefit.

Date _____, Office of Issue _____   Policy issued No. _____

This Certificate must be produced when cashing Postal Drafts and Army Money Orders for weekly pay whilst on furlough.

The Postmaster will stamp a ring for each payment made.   P.O. Stamp to be impressed here when Savings Bank Book is issued.

(1)

CERTIFICATE of * { ~~Discharge~~ Transfer to Reserve ~~Disembodiment~~ Demobilization } on Demobilization.   Army Form Z. 21.

Regtl. No. 227656. Rank. 1/A.M.

Names in full Gelsthorpe Gladwin Webster Thomas.
(Surname first)

Unit and Regiment or Corps
from which
* ~~Discharged~~
Transferred to Reserve } G } Royal Air Force

Enlisted on the 26th March 191 7

For Royal Naval Air Service
(Here state Regiment or Corps to which first appointed)

Also served in Royal Air Force

Only Regiments or Corps in which the Soldier served since August 4th, 1914, are to be stated. If inapplicable, this space is to be ruled through in ink and initialled.

† Medals and
Decorations
awarded during
present engagement } e Nil

~~Has~~
Has not } served Overseas on Active Service.

Place of Rejoining in }
case of emergency } Shrewsbury Medical Category. A

Specialist Military }
qualifications } Gardener Year of birth 1896

He is * { ~~Discharged~~ ~~Transferred to Army Reserve~~ ~~Disembodied~~ Demobilized } on 11th April 191 9
in consequence of Demobilization.

Signature and Rank.

Officer i/c Records. (Place)

* Strike out whichever is inapplicable. † The word "Nil" to be inserted when necessary.

W8225 P1336 250,000 12.18 HWV(P1386)

Office of Issue :—

HARROWBY

Policy $\frac{A}{26}$ N? 008442

Number _____ Rank _____

Name _____
    (In full, Christian names first. In the case of women state whether Mrs. or Miss)

Unit and Regiment _____

Date of Birth _____

Industrial Group _____

Trade _____

Classification No. _____

OUT-OF-WORK DONATION POLICY

(H.M. Forces).

This Policy is of no value except to the person to whom it is issued.
For Instructions and Conditions as to receipt of Out-of-Work Donation
see pages 2 and 4 of cover.

A | D. 3

Holder's Signature _____

The first date on which this Policy will be available is...........................
(this is the date on which the holder may begin to sign the coupons herein).

This Policy is available for twelve months from the end of furlough. Therefore, it will not be available after...........................

The number of weeks of donation which may be drawn up to and including the last above-mentioned date is twenty-six weeks at the rate of 24s. a week for men and 20s. a week for women, subject to the conditions printed on this Policy. A supplementary donation is payable in respect of dependent children under 15 years of age at the following rates per week :—

6s. for first child and 3s. in respect of each additional child.

HOW TO OBTAIN OUT-OF-WORK DONATION.

1. On becoming unemployed and desiring to obtain donation you must lodge this Policy at an Employment Exchange or at a Branch Employment Office of the Ministry of Labour. (The address of the nearest Exchange or Branch Office can be obtained at any Post Office.)

2. On attending at an Exchange or Branch Office to claim donation you must also take with you your discharge papers and there sign the form of claim to donation in this Policy.

3. So long as you are unemployed and desirous of drawing donation you must attend daily, or in certain exceptional cases less frequently, between certain hours which will be notified to you at an Exchange or Branch Office for the purpose of signing in this Policy a declaration of unemployment.

4. Until you desire to claim out-of-work donation you must retain this Policy in your own possession.

Week ending..................   **Policy** A / 56   No. 008442

I, the undersigned, hereby apply for out-of-work donation, being a person discharged from H.M. Forces. I hereby declare that (1) the undermentioned particulars are correct; (2) that I am the person named in the holder of this Policy, and that as regards each occasion of signature I am (3) unemployed and unable to obtain suitable employment; (4) capable of work and (5) that the conditions for the receipt of out-of-work donation as stated on this Policy are satisfied in my case. I further apply for supplementary donation in respect of .... living children, who are dependent upon me, and I declare that the information furnished in the statement as to children at the end of this Policy is true, and that no other person is applying for or receiving supplementary donation under the National Insurance (Unemployment) Acts, 1911 to 1918, in respect of the unemployment benefit under the National Insurance (Unemployment) Acts, 1911 to 1918, in respect of the period covered by this application, and am not in receipt of any out-of-work donation under any other scheme.

Last Employer ....   Business ....

Address ....

from .... till ....

Occupation ....

Check No. .... Foreman ....

Day of Week.	Policy Holder's Signature.	I. D. Stamp.	Code &c.
Wed.			
Thur.			
Fri.			
Sat.			
Mon.			
Tues.			

---

eek ending: 1

cal Office ....

o. of dependent children ....

	DAYS SIGNED :				
W.	Th.	F.	S	M.	T.

Days of donation already paid :

Days of donation paid on this coupon ....

ntered by ....

ecked by ....

AIR FORCE. No......*1629.35*......

      If you will now call at the

Hornsea Hull.

Post Office and produce your Protection
Certificate an account book numbered as
above will be issued to you.

        Should it be inconvenient to you
to attend at the office named you should
state on the back of this card to what office
you would like the book sent. If you have
removed, give new address. Then put the
card in an envelope addressed to

    The Controller,
      Post Office Savings Bank,
           London, W. 14.

O.H.M.S.
—

OFFICIAL PAID

Mrs S. W. Gilsthorpe
"Lunwoft"
Eastbourne Rd,
Hornsea
E. Yorks.

                                               M. 41

SPECIAL EMERGENCY CARD, SOLDIER OR SAILOR.

1. Holder *Gilsthorpe G 427656*
    (Name and Number)
2. Unit or Ship *Royal Air Force Hornsea*
3. Proceeding from *Hornsea* to *Leeds*
4. Beginning of leave *signal 23/9/18*
5. End of leave or duty *28/9/18*
6. Is holder proceeding at end of leave
    or duty on Active Service or
    Service afloat?
7. Signature of Officer issuing
8. Unit or Ship of Officer issuing

INSTRUCTIONS TO HOLDER.

1. Each butter and margarine coupon represents one week's ration. The meat coupons entitle you to purchase meat at a shop according to the official Table of Equivalent Weights displayed in the shop. Coupons marked "Other Meat Only" cannot ... be purchased anywhere. A ... or half coupon may be used only ... not used anywhere.

2. The card is not transferable. You must produce the card whenever you buy butter, margarine or the rationed meat. The seller will detach coupons.

3. You must obtain fresh coupons over the ... period of your leave and of your journey out and back. No fresh card will be issued to you unless the period of your leave ... days is exceeded. Should the ... you will take this card with the remaining coupons to the Relieving of leave or duty to the Local Food Office, who will issue you an Emergency Card to cover the remainder of your leave or duty. This card ceases to be valid at the expiration of your leave or duty as indicated by the date entered opposite 5 above.

PENALTIES FOR MISUSE.—£100 or six months' imprisonment, or both.

BUTCHER'S or OTHER MEAT	BUTCHER'S or OTHER MEAT	BUTCHER'S or OTHER MEAT	BUTCHER'S or OTHER MEAT
4 or 5	6 or 7	8 or 8	8 or 9

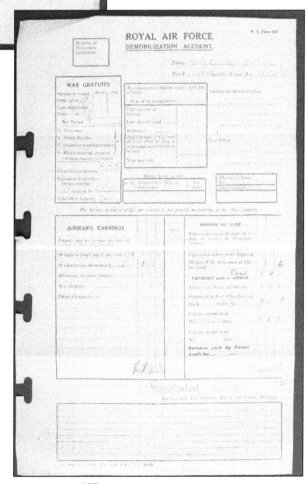

ROYAL AIR FORCE
DEMOBILIZATION ACCOUNT.

F. S. Form 637

Number of
Protection
Certificate

Name ....
Rank ....

WAR GRATUITY

Re-engagement Bounty under A.O. 28 of 1946 ....

Address on demobilization

Date of re-engagement ....

Full amount of Bounty ....

Less already paid ....

Difference ....

Post Office

AIRMAN'S EARNINGS.

Balance due to Airman on date of ....

28 days furlough pay to per rate ....

28 days ration allowance at ....

Allowance for plain clothes ....

War Gratuity ....

Other allowances ....

MANNER OF ISSUE

PAYMENTS made to AIRMAN

Advance at Dispersal station ....

Deposited in Post Office Savings Bank ... Acct. No. ....

Paid by postal draft ....

Balance paid by Postal draft No. ....

107

Leaflet 29a.
(Revised Dec. 1918.)

NATIONAL HEALTH INSURANCE.

INSURANCE OF DISCHARGED SOLDIERS AND AIRMEN.

(Discharge in this leaflet includes transfer to the reserve.)

BENEFITS :—

1. If you were insured in the Army or Air Force you will, subject to certain conditions, be entitled on discharge to the following benefits :—

MEDICAL BENEFIT, that is Doctor and Medicine ;

SANATORIUM BENEFIT, that is, Treatment in a Sanatorium or in some other way in case of tuberculosis.

MATERNITY BENEFIT, that is, 30s. on wife's confinement.

An insured person is not qualified for Maternity Benefit unless at the time of his wife's confinement he has been insured for 42 weeks and 42 contributions have been paid.

SICKNESS AND DISABLEMENT BENEFITS, that is, periodical payments during incapacity for work.

Sickness benefit is payable for a period or periods not exceeding 26 weeks in all for any one sickness. Two periods of sickness not separated by a period of at least twelve months count as one. The ordinary rate is 10s. a week, but until a man has been insured for 104 weeks and 104 weekly contributions have been paid, the rate is usually 6s. a week only.

Disablement benefit is a continuation of the periodical payments at a lower rate (ordinarily 5s. a week) after the period of sickness benefit has been exhausted.

A man does not become qualified for Sickness benefit until he has been insured for 26 weeks and 26 weekly contributions have been paid, or for disablement benefit until he has been insured for 104 weeks and 104 weekly contributions have been paid.

Discharge Postcard (Form O.1845).

2. You should receive on discharge Form O.1845 (buff coloured postcard) which is a certificate showing that you have been insured in the Army or Air Force, and giving the period of your service.

If you do not receive this postcard on or before getting your final balance of pay you should apply to your Regimental Paymaster for it, as without this postcard you may have difficulty in obtaining benefit when you require it. In case of necessity if the postcard has not been received you should show your discharge paper to the Society as evidence of your discharge, but on no account should you part with the discharge paper.

What to do with the Discharge Postcard (Form O.1845).

3. First of all write on it your name and address and particulars of your Approved Society as directed.

If you are a member of an Approved Society give or send it at once to the Secretary or to the local Agent of your Society. The name and address of your Society and your membership number can be obtained from your old Insurance Book or Record Card.

If you are not a member of an Approved Society send the postcard to the Navy and Army Insurance Fund, National Health Insurance Commission, Maida Hill, London, W.9.

Uninsured Men.

14. If you were not insured during service but are certified by the proper authorities to be suffering on discharge from any disease or bodily or mental disablement you are entitled to medical and sanatorium benefits provided your income from all sources does not exceed £160 a year.

The arrangements for providing these benefits are the same as in paragraph 5 (a) above. If you do not receive a medical attendance voucher under the arrangements described in that paragraph you may make application for one to the local Insurance Committee (see Note 2 below), stating whether you have been awarded a pension, gratuity or allowance in respect of disablement. When writing to the Committee state the name of your regiment, your regimental number, and the date and cause of your discharge.

Invalided Men in Ireland.

15. Medical benefit under the Insurance Acts is not given in Ireland, but if you are discharged from His Majesty's Forces as unfit for further service during the present War you are entitled to receive medical attendance and treatment under a scheme administered by the Irish Insurance Commissioners on behalf of the Minister of Pensions.

If you are an invalided man resident in Ireland the Irish Insurance Commissioners will send you, shortly after your discharge, a medical card which will enable you to get treatment and medical certificates free of charge. If you do not receive such a medical card within ten days of your discharge you should write to the Irish Insurance Commissioners, Pembroke House, Upper Mount Street, Dublin, giving your full name, address, pension number, name of your late regiment, &c., your regimental number, and the date and cause of your discharge.

NOTES:—

1. A List of Approved Societies can be seen at any Labour Exchange or Public Library.

2. A List of doctors through whom medical benefit is obtainable can be seen at any Post Office in England, Scotland and Wales; this List also contains the address of the local Insurance Committee.

3. All communications to the Navy and Army Insurance Fund should be addressed to the Secretary, National Health Insurance Commission, (Navy and Army Insurance Fund), Maida Hill, London, W.9.

NATIONAL HEALTH INSURANCE COMMISSION,
December, 1918.

4913. Wt. /G6945. 5,000,000(?) 12/18. S.O., F.Bd.

How to Get a Contribution Card.

4. When sending Form O.1845 to your Society ask the Secretary or Agent for a contribution card to hand to your employer.

If you are not a member of an Approved Society a card will be sent to you from the Navy and Army Insurance Fund as soon as you send in Form O.1845.

How to Get Medical Benefit.

5. (a) If invalided—

If you were discharged on account of medical unfitness you should receive on discharge a Medical Attendance Voucher (Form I.S.1.). On taking this to a doctor you can obtain Medical Benefit at once. If by any chance you do not receive a Form I.S.1 in the ordinary course, you can get one by applying to the local Insurance Committee (whose address can be obtained at any Post Office), giving the name of your regiment, your regimental number, and the date and cause of your discharge as shown on your Discharge Paper. These arrangements apply to Great Britain only; for Ireland see paragraph 15.

(b) If not invalided—

If you were not discharged on account of medical unfitness you should when sending in Form O.1845 ask the Secretary or Agent of your Approved Society to arrange with the local Insurance Committee for a medical card to be sent to you.

If you are not a member of an Approved Society, either the Navy and Army Insurance Fund or the Deposit Contributors Fund, as the case may be (see paragraphs 12 and 13), will arrange for a medical card to be sent to you by the local Insurance Committee.

In case of urgency you may (whether a member of an Approved Society or not) apply for a medical card to the local Insurance Committee on Form Med. 30, which can be obtained at any Post Office.

Immediately you get the medical card take it to the Insurance Doctor from whom you wish to receive treatment when ill.

How to Get Sanatorium Benefit.

6. Special arrangements are in force for giving to tuberculous discharged men residential treatment immediately on discharge where such treatment is essential.

But any discharged man who is suffering from tuberculosis may, and should in his own interest, at once apply to the local Insurance Committee for sanatorium benefit. This may take the form of residential treatment in an institution, or of treatment at a dispensary or in the patient's own home.

How to Get Sickness Benefit.

7. When you are incapable of work ask your doctor to give you a medical certificate. Fill in the right hand portion of the form on which the certificate is given, and send it to your Approved Society, or if you are a member of the Navy and Army Insurance Fund, to the local Insurance Committee. The first certificate should be sent to the Society or Committee within three days after the commencement of the incapacity, as sickness benefit is not payable in respect of a period before you give notice of incapacity unless you are able to satisfy your Society or Committee that you could not reasonably give notice earlier. Medical certificates should be furnished even although you may be in receipt of a pension in respect of 100 per cent. disablement. (See paragraph 8.)

Note—A discharged man may have a pension for wounds, etc., without being incapable of work, but he must be incapable of work before he can get sickness benefit.

Effect of a Pension or Gratuity in respect of "100 per cent." Disablement in Consequence of the War.

8. If you are granted a *pension* for disablement in the highest degree, i.e., 100 per cent., on account of injuries or disease due to the War (not less than 27s. 6d. a week, excluding allowances for children), you will, as a condition attaching to the pension (but only as long as you continue to receive it), have your ordinary rate of sickness benefit reduced by 5s. a week until you have again since your discharge been in insurable employment for 26 weeks and 26 weekly contributions have been paid, and you will not be entitled to any disablement benefit until you have again since your discharge been in insurable employment for 104 weeks and 104 weekly contributions have been paid. If you are granted an *allowance in lieu of pension* during treatment or training the same conditions apply as long as the allowance continues.

If you are awarded a *gratuity* of £30 or more in place of a pension, any portion of which is in respect of temporary total disablement, you will not be entitled to any sickness or disablement benefit until you have again since your discharge been in insurable employment for 26 weeks and 26 weekly contributions have been paid in respect of you. The gratuity awarded will be fixed to include 26 weeks sickness benefit. If at a later date you are awarded a pension your position will be determined by reference to the rate of pension; if you are awarded a pension in respect of disablement in the highest degree the arrangements in the foregoing paragraph will apply, but if you receive a pension for disablement in a lower degree your right to benefit will not be affected by your pension.

No reduction in the rate of sickness or disablement benefit is made in the case of pensions or gratuities for disablement in a lower degree or for disablement not due to the War.

Free Year's Insurance.

9. If you have been insured in the Army or Air Force, but do not become employed and insured after discharge, you will be entitled to all benefits for a limited period. If you are a member of a Society or of the Navy and Army Insurance Fund you will be entitled to all benefits, subject to the provisions as to arrears, for at least a year from date of discharge, when your membership of the Society or of the Navy and Army Insurance Fund will cease. You will, however, be entitled to receive medical and sanatorium benefit until the end of the calendar year in which your membership ceases. If you are a deposit contributor you will be entitled, on application, to medical and sanatorium benefits for a limited period of about a year, and to other benefits to a limited amount, as explained in paragraph 13; you will then cease to be a deposit contributor.

Voluntary Contributors.

10. If you have been insured for 104 weeks whether in the Army or Air Force or as a contributor in civil life, you may continue in insurance as a voluntary contributor if you give notice to the Society of which you are a member, or to the Navy and Army Insurance Fund if you are a member of that Fund, of your desire to do so before the date on which your membership would otherwise cease.

Discharged Men who are Not Members of any Approved Society.

11. If you are not a member of an Approved Society you will, on sending in Form O.1845 to the Navy and Army Insurance Fund receive a form of enquiry to fill up in order that it may be decided whether you are entitled to benefits out of the Navy and Army Insurance Fund or must be a Deposit Contributor.

The Navy and Army Insurance Fund.

12. If on discharge you are certified by the proper authorities to be suffering from any disease or disablement, or bodily or mental unfitness, you will be entitled to benefits out of the Navy and Army Insurance Fund, but if your incapacity is due to some minor ailment you may be called upon as a condition of continued membership of the Fund to satisfy the Fund that your state of health would prevent you from obtaining admission to an Approved Society.

If you are admitted to the Navy and Army Insurance Fund detailed instructions will be sent to you as to your position as a member.

The Deposit Contributors Fund.

13. If you have not been certified to be suffering from disease or disablement, or bodily or mental unfitness on discharge, you will be a deposit contributor unless you join an Approved Society or unless within six months from your discharge, you prove that the state of your health is such that you cannot obtain admission to an Approved Society. An account will be opened for you in the Deposit Contributors Fund if you have sent in your discharge password (Form O.1845) and furnished all further information required. You will then receive a medical card entitling you to medical benefit from the date of its issue, and you will also be entitled to other benefits, subject to the usual conditions, but only so far as the cash value of the contributions to your credit permits. If, however, you are qualified for maternity benefit and make a claim within a year of your discharge the full sum of 30s. will be paid.

A man who on discharge has not been certified to be suffering from disease or disablement or bodily or mental unfitness, but who within six months from discharge proves that the state of his health is such that he cannot obtain admission to an Approved Society is entitled to benefits out of the Navy and Army Insurance Fund.

The full advantage of National Health Insurance can only be obtained by becoming a member of an Approved Society or of the Navy and Army Insurance Fund. You should, therefore, apply to an Approved Society for admission without loss of time after discharge, and if you are rejected on account of the state of your health write to the Navy and Army Insurance Fund as soon as possible, but, in any case, not later than six months from the date of your discharge.

111

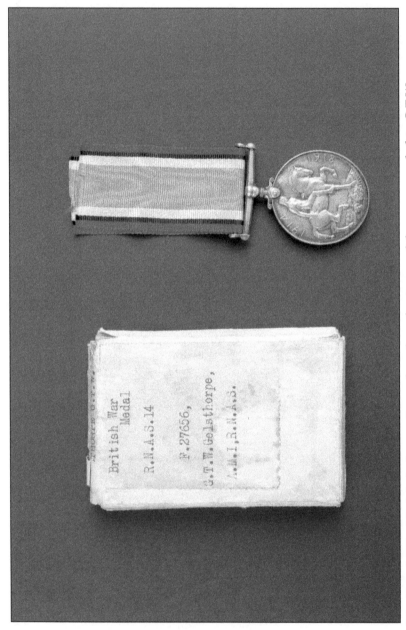

The British War Medal. As he was home-based, no foreign medals were awarded to G.T.W.

Details from British Royal Air Force, Airmen's Service Records, 1912-1939, are listed here.

Official Number:	227656
Christian Names:	Gladwin Thomas Webster
Surname:	Gelsthorpe
Birth:	27th April 1890
Town:	Nottingham
Parish:	Hucknall
County:	Nottinghamshire
Current Engagement in H.M. Forces:	Navy
Period: Man Service:	26th March 1917
Date of Actual Entry into the R.N.A.S.:	26th March 1917
Civilian Occupation:	Carpenter and Joiner
Person to be informed of casualties:	Thomas
Address:	Rose Villa, Healing, Lincolnshire
Relationship:	Father
Height:	5ft 7 5/8 inches
Chest	38 ¼ inches
Hair:	Black
Eyes:	R Hazel, L Brown
Complexion:	Fresh

Marks wounds or scars:
   Scar: Centre forehead
   Scar: Right thumb
   Scar: Left index finger.

Transfer to R.A.F. Reserve:	6th April 1919 DRO 148th
Discharge:	30 April 1920
Address on discharge:	Suncroft, Hornsea, Yorks
Movements:	Hornsea, 1.4.18, Air Mechanic 1(C) 26.1.17
	Transfer to R.A.F. 1.4.1918

Medical Boards	DRO/148	Cat A	6.4.1919

9. Missing Photographs

G.T.W. was a keen photographer and he took numerous photographs during his service years. This book has examples of these but unfortunately his large box of negatives were loaned out and have not been returned. It would be interesting to find those now.

Joe Gelsthorpe, Hornsea (01964) 535201